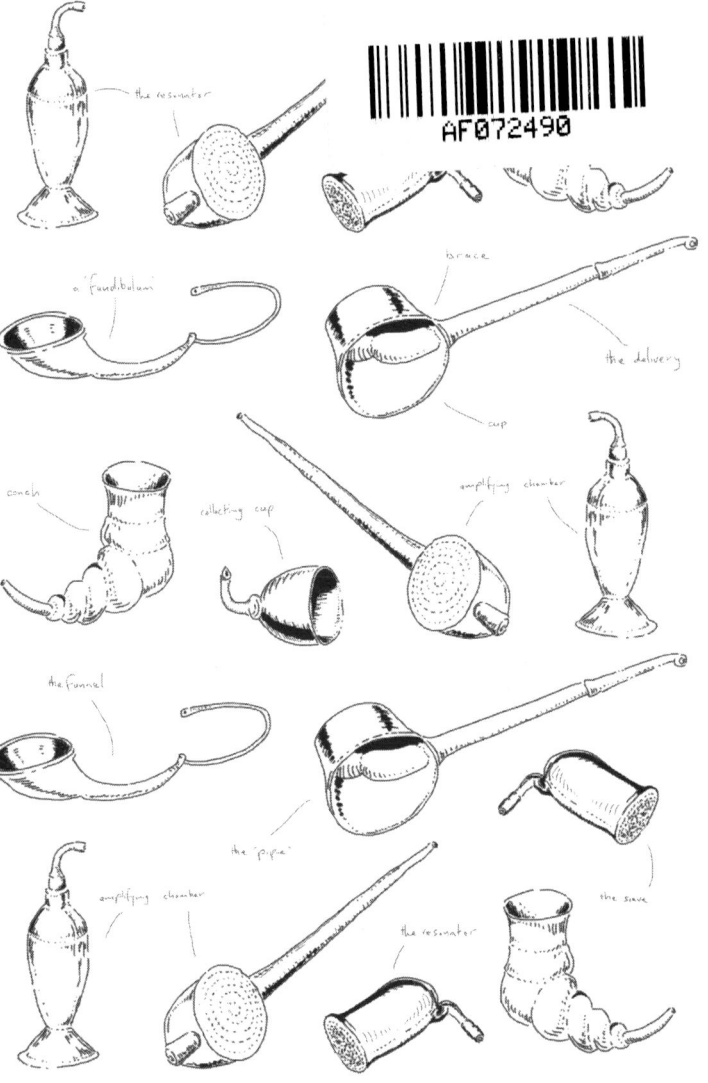

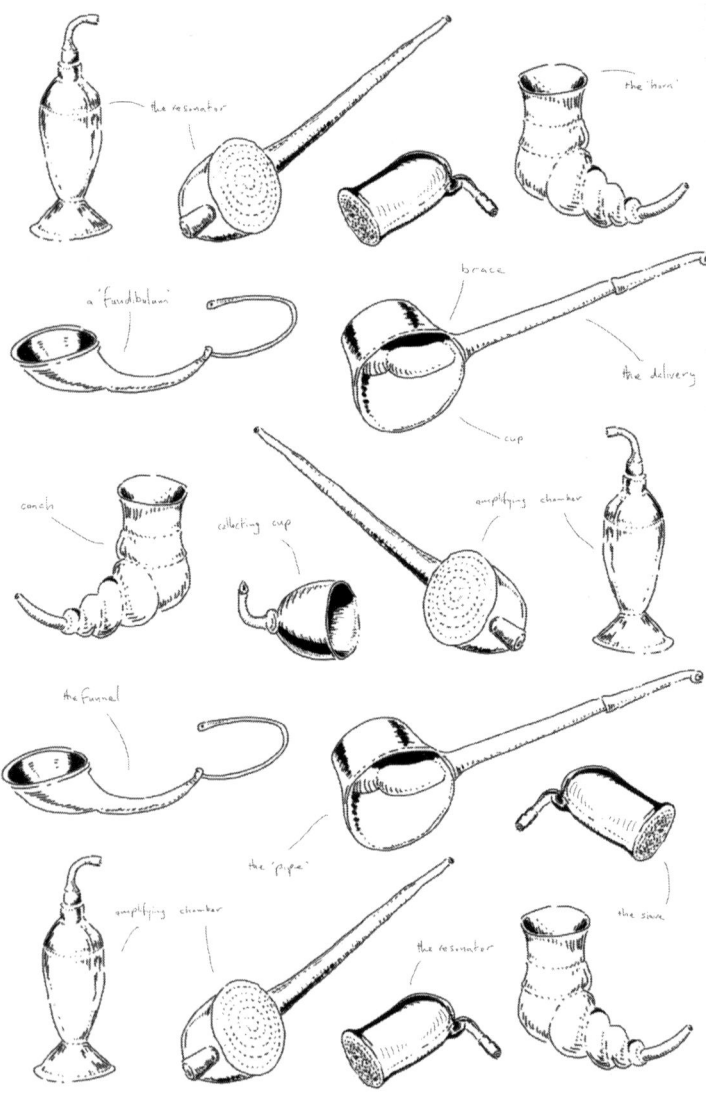

PHILIP LEVINE'S GOOD EAR

Lisa Kelly

Stonewood
THUMBPRINTS

First published in 2018
by Stonewood Press
Diversity House
72 Nottingham Road, Arnold
Nottingham NG5 6LF
books@stonewoodpress.co.uk
www.stonewoodpress.co.uk

All rights reserved
Poems © Lisa Kelly, 2018
The author asserts her moral right to be
identified as the author of this work

ISBN: 978-1-910413-29-6 (paperback)
ISBN: 978-1-910413-30-2 (ebook)

Represented by Inpress
0191 230 8104
customerservices@inpressbooks.co.uk

Printed and bound in the UK by Imprintdigital, Exeter

Designed and typeset in Minion 10.5pt/12.5pt
by www.silbercow.co.uk
Cover illustration and endpapers by Martin Parker

This is the seventh book in the THUMBPRINT series

ACKNOWLEDGEMENTS

A huge thanks to the Torriano Meeting House Thursday Poetry Group and to all the poets who share their work, insight and give support on Sunday evenings at the Torriano; to Jacqueline Gabbitas and Martin Parker for their extraordinary care in helping craft this Thumbprint; and to the D/deaf poets, writers, audience and supporters who helped make *Magma* 69, The Deaf Issue, happen.

The following poems have appeared (some in different versions) in: Ø – *Interpreter's House*, # 56, 'Aubade for an Artist' – *Under the Radar*, Summer 2016, 'Saltatorium' and 'Polar Observations with Anagram Shadows' – *Brittle Star*, Issue 41, 'Ghost Heritage' – *Brittle Star*, Issue 38, 'Herring Loss' – *Antiphon*, Issue 17, 'Philip Levine's Good Ear' – *Antiphon*, Issue 20, 'A&E' – *The Spectator,* 'Obelus' – appeared in the anthology *Asterism* (Laudanum), 'Aphid Reproduction as Unpunctuated White Noise' – appeared in *New Poetries VII* (Carcanet), 'Herring Loss' appeared in the Nine Arches Press anthology *Stairs and Whispers: D/deaf and Disabled Poets Write Back.*

CONTENTS

Aubade for an Artist	7
Ø	8
Ghost Heritage	10
Philip Levine's Good Ear	11
Saltatorium	12
How to Explain Melodious	13
Lady Monoaural	14
Knag	16
Colchester Native	17
The Sound of Thunder in the Night	18
Herring Loss	19
Slant of Summer	20
A&E	21
Deaf Wannabe	22
Polar Observations with Anagram Shadows	23
Aphid Reproduction and Unpunctuated White Noise	24
Deaf Dance	26
The Flesh Made Mobile	27
÷	28

AUBADE FOR AN ARTIST

Of course the morning came; it always does,
but before was an evening, and it was
such an evening I felt already afraid
of morning before the light began to fade.

He cooked while I looked out of a sash window.
As he set the table, I said, *There's a rainbow*,
and he replied, *I painted the sky for you*.
Such a perfect response: too good to be true.

So we ate, and I remember it was fish,
which I don't much like, but again the dish
of tarnished silver was so perfectly placed
on a crushed red velvet curtain, draped

over a folding table in the room's centre
that the flavour meant less than the gesture,
the blunt edge, notched tip of a fish knife –
I thought, *Can we possibly still our lives*.

Of course the morning came; it always does,
but before was an evening, and it was
such an evening I felt already afraid
of morning before the light began to fade.

Ø

Danish for island
a new word
new world
to explore

My tongue
tastes the sound of Ø
touches its shores
its limits

I dream of Ø, wishing
it in my blood
as the English sound
that comes so easily it is thoughtless

Ø floats
like those white blood cells
that gave my mother
& her tongue life

My mouth has a Caliban look
monsterish in expressiveness
and more ridiculously
round than Ø

Surrounded by a sea of white
Ø is what it means
but I can't possess
even this small word

The axis cutting
north-east to south-west
makes Ø
a *No Entry* sign

I will navigate Ø
the line going through
is a river perhaps
and will lead to fresh water

GHOST HERITAGE

Bisect me: discover my left eardrum lined with rockwool.
In my home town there are whispers picked up by my right ear:
fears about school places, pressure on housing;
it hears every nuance of Englishness, the right
to speak in red and white of discomfort and disjointedness.

The whisperers don't know my left ear's deaf; insulated
against whitevan noise and exhaust; insulated against
my mother tongue. Don't know my mother was an immigrant;
that when they whisper I feel discomfort and disjointedness.
They don't know I'm half Danish, half deaf. Why would they?

PHILIP LEVINE'S GOOD EAR

Your poem, 'Nightship' starts with "Ceuta", how you said you'd like to go there. I'm not sure how to pronounce Ceuta, but try Kay-tə, never having been, and not knowing how to approach a strange Spanish word with my stupid tongue. If someone could sound it out slow and sure, I would not necessarily remember. I know this, because someone did, and I don't. It's in my head you say it: Say-uu-tə or maybe Sew-tə. Sounds come and go, some dock and some, like your ship, sail on. In your poem, the ticket seller's clock is stuck at quarter-to-three, and of course clock rhymes with dock, but there are no clues about what might rhyme with Ceuta, although this would not help with the back-of-the-throat v. tongue/teeth approach to the opening syllable and is not something to get hung up on. Your thought, *Africa, a whole new world!* is probably a key moment for many readers, but apart from the fear of stumbling over Ceuta my interest is in what you hear – the three layers of sound: water crashing into the hull & beneath that the steady beating of the engine & beneath that the wind whispering "Ceuta" into your good ear. This is what I leave with from your poem – your sensitivity to timbres of sound and a shared good ear. My deaf ear says Kay-tə, my good ear says if the wind whispers it must be Say-uu-tə or Sew-tə. Your last line gives away nothing: Starless, the sky gave away nothing.

SALTATORIUM

O drear, O dreary dreary dirge for this deer
that hath stallèd in a ditch all anitch with fear,
and how it twitch, how it fidget and flinch
its formerly fine fetlock, fends off the dog howls,
fends off the fender of the four-by-four Ford,
fleeing its flightpath, shit trails like smoke trails
like entrails. Haven't you, though, haven't you
sometimes in a sensitive somewhat sensory
rush hour of solemnity sensed its shadow?
This is no laughing matter, this is no ha-ha
wall at the Hameau de la Reine as grass grazes
garden, and your gaze graces a deer-leap into space.
This is its history, its ditch down, your disown.
Buckshot. *For 2 miles*, forever. Fallow migration.

HOW TO EXPLAIN MELODIOUS

How close, if notes are missed,
is melody to malady, how nearly
a hair's breadth touches a hare's breath

if the rhythm of tyre on tarmac is missed;
how missing Melody off the list to the party,
might make us sing without melody.

How melody did not exist for the girl
who hid in the cupboard under the stairs
to make believe she was under the stars,

sick of the here and now, the throb
of the entertainer and his cretinous hare
with a hand for a brain. How he could not hear

what she heard, how close melodious is
to malodorous, the reek of his sweat, his breath
as he tried to make a poppet laugh at a puppet.

There were no musical instruments,
he blew a kazoo made from tissue paper,
folded over a comb.

LADY MONOAURAL

after Elizabeth Bishop's 'The Gentleman of Shalott'

"Half is enough,"
she wishes to be quoted as saying at present:
that sense of constant re-adjustment
she loves, finds exhilarating
the uncertainty –
and her ear can clasp
another sound.
She can talk and run rings around
while a mouth stays put,
only one ear, etc.
she's in a fix –
if the mouth slips
but to such economical design
she's resigned.

Thought, she thinks, might be affected,
if half her ear's refracted,
but there's no proof, either.
There's little margin for error.
A mirror image,
but as to which side is in or out,
she's in no doubt.
Down the edge, or rather
down her middle

the impasse must stretch.
For why should she be doubted,
half-hearing loss
her person was
she felt in modesty.

Of what we realign,
somewhere along the line
of a mithered reflection,
it's the indication
to her mind.
Ear and so on,
of good ear and deaf ear and
in this arrangement
nor hears a stranger
nor the other,
nor a different holler
for neither is clearer.
Next the mirror,
which ear lies?
Which ear's her ear?

KNAG

Not the nag *do this*, *do that*,
not the nag fit for the knacker,
but knag as in knot – not the not in
'not the nag *do this*, *do that*'
nor the not in 'not the nag fit for the knacker',
but the knot in wood or a short projection
from the trunk – a dead branch or dead wood
like my dead ear is a knag, a short projection
that hasn't the knack – that's *knack* not knag –
to hear the nag *do this*, *do that* however projected;
a knag fit for the knacker.

COLCHESTER NATIVE

after the installation by Dallas Pierce Quintero

Oysters shucked. Poor man's beef discarded
down guts and out again to sea. Shells salvaged.
Here, concentrated behind wire mesh, hard stuffing
for this upholstered seat placed for musing
on the curve of the river Colne. Quantities shipped
to satiate Elizabethan London gullets.
The centre sucking resources in greedy gulps.
Local beds, and locals lay wasted in leaner times.
What now? Lean back on shells, characteristically
flat, the flesh enjoyed by Romans firm and salty,
a wet dream of these parts. Orgiastic oysters,
slipping down, coming up, their stockmarket fortunes,
bivalve biology, always two sides to prise apart:
rich & poor, insider & outsider. Pearly junkets
or gritty chronicles? Filter feeders, take it all in and sift
through for dignitaries at the annual Oyster Feast
by invitation only since Saint Dennis held his fair.
Left out in the cold, sit back, digest world wars
and viruses, how oyster numbers could not atone:
oistre, ostreum, ostreon. Osteon, so close to bone.

THE SOUND OF THUNDER IN THE NIGHT

The thunder sounded like a van door sliding
back or a giant metal sheet shook out –
at one point that is; at another point
the thunder sounded like a baby's heart beating
under a stethoscope or the grumble of a train,
then at a certain point the thunder sounded
like a chisel cracking quartz, or *What?*
swallowed by a throat. At no point did the thunder
sound like you shifting to lie on your good ear.

HERRING LOSS

Half heard, now half remembered
what was it I thought you said
as I beg my brain for the word I know
begins with *b*? The sense of something
on the tip of my tongue, which lurks
behind bottom teeth as lips purse *b*
goldfishing empty speech bubbles.

The Christmas cracker joke you told,
*What did the fish say when he swam
into a wall?* has an in-built sinker,
if not the right line, hooking *codswallop*,
all manner of red herrings, as I bang
my head against a brick wall, and hit
upon it was not *b* but *d. Damn!*

SLANT OF SUMMER

There's a black and white photo of my half-siblings
stuck in my memory, their legs in wooden stocks.
My sister's head is tilted. She is half-smiling.
The white bow in her hair matches her white dress,
although what is white could be pink or powder green
in that slant of summer. Our brother, laid-back,
leans away from the lens. This is his time to dream,
fringe falling over one eye, on half-term break
from boarding school, where he was force-fed maggots
and sat half-asleep to warm the toilet seat
for a prick of a prefect, and there's a cuteness-
cum-cockiness in his eye which might or might not
antagonise the man who will cuckold his father –
who may or may not already be part of the picture.

A&E

If this waiting is hellish, then the sick are limbo dancing;
only those who are bent double, or on the floor, puddles
of their former selves, have a hope of getting under the bar,
progressively lowered as more contorted squeeze through.

If the woman in a white coat is god, then the boy with bleeding
hands has stigmata, the man on the stretcher is Lazarus,
and the toddler pushing donkey-on-wheels up and down,
up and down, is one of the Four Horsemen of the Apocalypse.

If this is a place of worship, then the grey kidney dishes
are donation plates passed for contributions from the faithful,
hopeful they are worth saving. If this is where you think the wait
will end in four hours, think again, the end is always waiting.

DEAF WANNABE

Not hard of hearing, he hurts
for a hearing aid, hopes to hijack the test,
put the wool in the audiologist's ear.

All those silent k words in his life:
the knots that tied his tongue,
unknowable knows, knights riding in nightmares –
he heard them all, repeated in a stutter:

k-k-k Not k-k-k Now k-k-k Night

He has heard all objections to obstructions:
glue, wax, oil, cotton, foam, but still he is hoarding
glue, wax, oil, cotton, foam, and repeating
glue, wax, oil, cotton, foam until it's a litany.

In his bedroom, he is cranking up the volume,
headbanging to perforated drums, over and over,
over and over, over and out.

At the bar, he is trying out a deaf voice,
trying out Ménière's Disease, trying out tinnitus,
trying to let someone hear his inner voice. *Listen,
listen how I hurt, listen how I harm, I can list
all the times when no one has listened.*

POLAR OBSERVATIONS WITH ANAGRAM SHADOWS

The moon is a hazy bitch.[1]
The underbelly of the Boeing is red.[2]
Don't say that swallow is a crossbow.[3]

A hibachi zest moth yon.
Heterogeneously hefted blind rib.
Switchboards swallow assay on tot.

---

1 My scuffed white boots kick asphalt.
2 My toenails are raspberry rippled.
3 Don't say that fly is a toering gem.

Wastebaskets thickly cuff mid hoop.
Inappropriately remarry blessed.
Day fogs intermittently oh saga.

APHID REPRODUCTION AND
UNPUNCTUATED WHITE NOISE

.

a full stop is an aphid not a comma nor an embryo
an aphid is a full stop is a nymph not a womb holding
a comma nor a question mark asks nothing of a slash
or a backslash bulges with parentheses bears
afterthought after afterthought as a full stop
parthenogenetic filled with full stops without
stopping without comma without pausing full stop
after full stop never comma not a comma until
all the space is taken with full stop upon full stop
not a comma and a full stop develops wings flies off

!

an exclamation mark is an aphid on the wing not a
full stop not a comma nor an embryo an aphid is
an exclamation mark not a womb holding a comma
nor a question mark asks nothing of a slash or a
backslash bulges with parentheses bears afterthought
after afterthought as a full stop parthenogenetic
not an exclamation mark not a comma but a full stop
filled with exclamation marks filled with full stops
bears exclamation marks filled with full stops
until summer heat has happened and love is in the air

.

an aphid is a male on the wing not a full stop
is an exclamation mark and an aphid is a female
on the wing not a full stop is an exclamation mark
gives birth to a full stop without wings mates
with an exclamation mark and lays a full stop
a full stop is an egg not an aphid but an egg
and the egg it is dormant is a full stop not a pause
not a comma nor an embryo but a full stop in the winter
without wings an egg is a full stop until spring
and it hatches a full stop is an aphid not a full stop

DEAF DANCE

You're on my left side, my bad side, my deaf side,
I demi do-si-do so we're shoulder to shoulder
with you on my right side, my good side, my hear side,
I sidestep the conference, the pub, the club,
now you're on the inside, and I'm on the outside,
we message in the middle: Whisky, Tango, Foxtrot!
You take the lead, and I try to follow,
turn your head and I'm left in a spin,
but I regain my balance – my ear's back in
for a cross-body lead and a final fandango:
cha-cha-cha, blah blah blah, time to step out solo,
I moontalk like Jacko and flail on the spot,
do the heel-toe-shuffle, and the mouth-ear-muffle
to the sound of one hand clapping, a headbanging stop.

THE FLESH MADE MOBILE

Wait until the music's loud enough,
the alcohol's rendered guests insensate:
soon we'll all be half deaf, half coherent,
unable to use a fork or a phone.

How many times has someone mistaken
my leaning in as an attempt to get amorous,
run fingers through hair, get a phone number?
Best just to smile, nod and eat.

Best just to eat. Like the time I finished off
the cheesecake at the golf club on my last day
waitressing, after a client's tantrum: I ordered
a cheese board. *Are you deaf or something?*

O my deaf ear. My hostess
approaches: *Have you got a knife 'n' for'?*
No, I'm alright with my fingers.
She asks my neighbour the same question:

Have you got an iPhone 4? I'm balancing
sausages, roly-poly tomatoes, (she needs
a compatible phone to get this party started),
a thin-stemmed glass of fizz, a paper plate.

This is our event horizon, the sun a black dot
ogling its reflection in the ocean of it all,

the line one of us crossed, obol on tongue,
the other an observer light cannot reach,

sucked in so far, returning is oblivion,
going over a spurious passage.

This is our event horizon, you horizontal,
my head hanging over yours,

a petrified intention to kiss,

the head in the golden round, divided,
each must have an eye, each a tooth.

This is our event horizon, the spot excised,
a hole stitched over, the slub in the thread

warping the line. Janus crosses the threshold,
unable to face the future, oblivious of the past.

Lisa Kelly is half Danish and has single-sided deafness from childhood mumps. She is a regular host of poetry evenings at the Torriano Meeting House in London and is Chair of *Magma Poetry* magazine. Her pamphlet *Bloodhound* was published by Hearing Eye in 2012. Poems have appeared in magazines and anthologies including *Carcanet's New Poetries VII*. Her debut collection *A Map Towards Fluency* is forthcoming from Carcanet in 2019.

If you've appreciated and enjoyed this book, perhaps you'd like to write a review for us either on Stonewood's own website at www.stonewoodpress.co.uk or on the seller's website if you bought it elsewhere.

Other Stonewood Press Thumbprints:

When You Lived Inside The Walls and other stories
by Krishan Coupland

A Massacre of Hummingbirds by Paul Blake

Green City by Sue MacIntyre

Dad's slideshow by Di Slaney

Hoad and other stories by Sarah Passingham

Earthworks by Jacqueline Gabbitas

www.stonewoodpress.co.uk

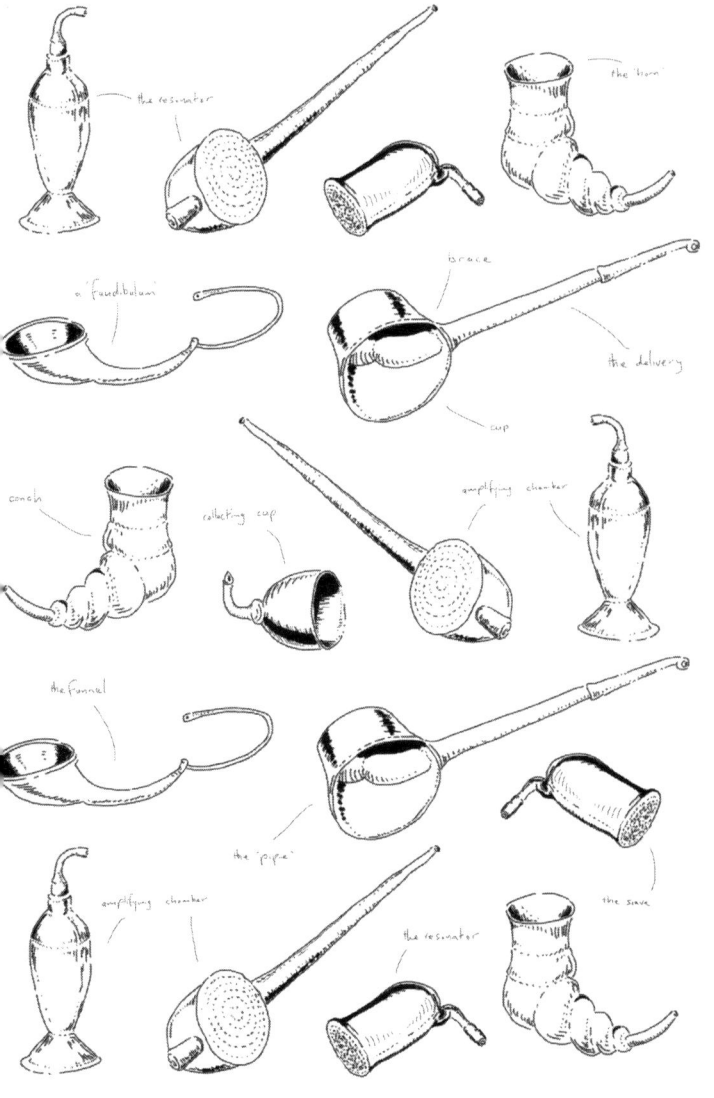

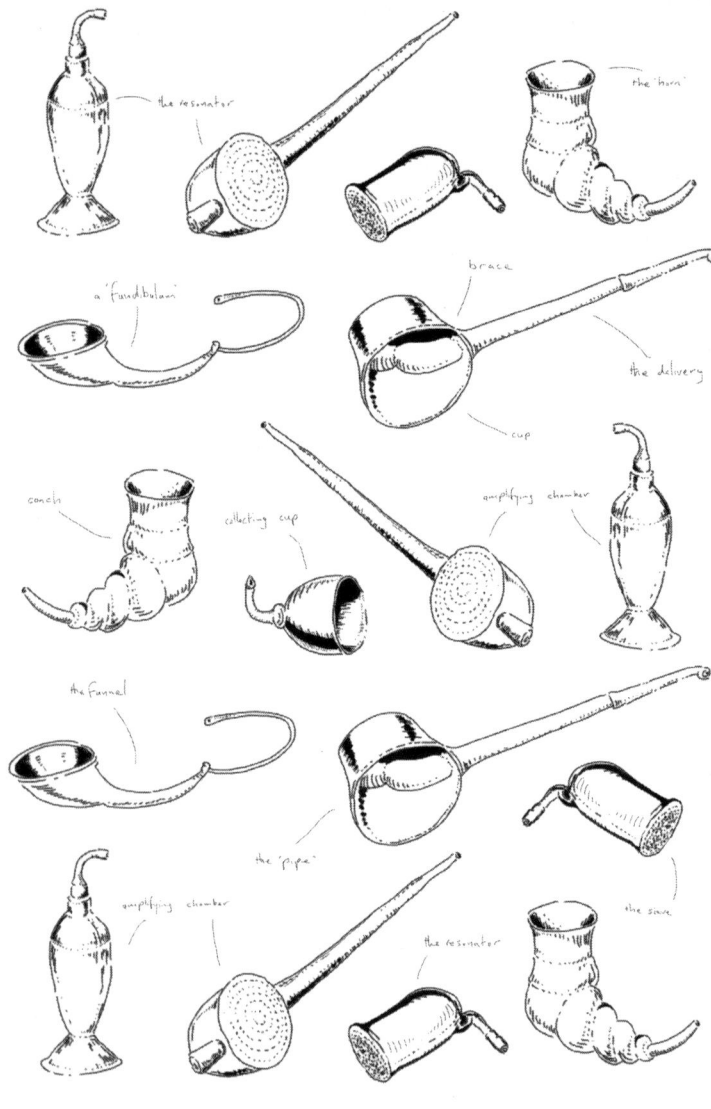